The
DEAN'S
LIST

The DEAN'S LIST

A Celebration of
Tar Heel Basketball
and Dean Smith

Art Chansky

Foreword by Michael Jordan

WARNER BOOKS

A Time Warner Company

PHOTO CREDITS

Hugh Morton—Pages 1, 2 (2), 3 (2), 4 (insets), 5, 7, 11, 13, 14, 15, 20, 21 (upper), 24, 33, 45 (insets), 46, 56 (lower), 74, 75, 76, 81 (3), 82 (2), 83, 84, 85, 91 (2), 94, 95 (lower), 96, 97 (2), 100, 104 (upper), 107 (left upper, right lower), 108 (insets), 109, 110 (2), 111 (upper), 112, 113 (lower), 115, 117, 118 (upper), 126 (2), 127 (2), 136 (2), 137, 138, 139 (lower), 141 (2), 142, 143, 144 (lower), 148 (upper), 152; **Bob Donnan**—iii, vii, 4, 6, 72, 90, 107 (2), 111 (lower), 113 (upper), 114, 119 (lower), 121 (upper), 122, 123, 124, 131 (2), 132, 133, 135, 139 (upper), 140; **Sally Sather**—89 (lower right), 92, 94 (upper), 98, 99 (upper), 108, 118 (2), 121 (lower); **Rich Clarkson**—9 (upper right), 25, 32, 36 (3), 63, 69; **Robert Crawford**—129; **Art Chansky**—9 (2); **Courtesy of Dr. Lou Vine**—14 (upper); **North Carolina Collection, UNC Library**—16; **Official White House Photograph**—viii; *Sports Illustrated*—57 (cover), 69 (Rich Clarkson), 83 (cover), 100 (cover), 142 (cover), 102 (Manny Millan), 150 (upper, Rich Clarkson); **Mark Dolejs/*Durham Herald-Sun***—144 (upper), 145 (2), 148; **Bernard Thomas/*Durham Herald-Sun***—149 (2); **Scott Sharpe/*Raleigh News & Observer***—106, 147; **Associated Press**—146, 150 (lower); **Courtesy of UNC Sports Information Office**—*Herald-Sun*/Charles Cooper 30, 31, 42, 45, 46 (middle inset); *Herald-Sun*/Harold Moore 25, 62, 99 (lower); *Herald-Sun*/Tony Rumple 17; *Herald-Sun*/Jim Sparks 34, 44 (lower), 46 (upper inset); *Fayetteville Observer-Times*/Ken Cooke 86; *Danville Bee*/John Hamlin 104; G. Thomas Barnes 93, 95 (upper); Tommy Esteridge 46 (lower inset), 49, 51, 52, 53; Jeep Hunter 48; Tom Maguire 83 (lower); Tom Norby 70; Tom Schnabel 65; Al Steele 103; Unidentified—8, 10 (2), 15, 18 (2), 19, 21, 23, 27, 28, 29, 35, 36 (lower left), 37, 39, 44 (upper), 47, 50, 54, 55 (2), 56 (upper), 60, 61, 64, 67, 73, 74 (inset), 75, 76 (inset), 78 (2), 79 (2), 87, 88, 89 (insets), 106.

Warner Books, Inc., 1271 Avenue of the Americas, New York, NY 10020

W A Time Warner Company

Printed in the United States of America
First Printing: October 1996
10 9 8 7 6 5 4

Library of Congress Cataloging-in-Publication Data
Chansky, Art.
    The Dean's list : a celebration of Tar Heel basketball and Dean
Smith / Art Chansky.
       p.   cm.
    Includes index.
    ISBN 0-446-52007-1
    1. Smith, Dean, 1931–   . 2. North Carolina Tar Heels (Basketball
team) 3. Basketball coaches—North Carolina—Biography.   I. Title.
GV884.S54C43   1996
796.323'092—dc20
[B]   96-15155
                                                                       CIP

Book design by H Roberts Design

ACKNOWLEDGMENTS

For me, writing a book about the last 35 years of Carolina basketball under Coach Dean Smith was not as difficult as one might imagine. You see, I have *lived* this story since arriving in Chapel Hill as a student during the 1960s.

First as a writer for the *Daily Tar Heel* and later as sports editor of the *Durham Morning Herald,* I have covered Carolina closely with both my head and my heart. From that time, Eddie Fogler has been a best friend, and picking up anecdotes and insights from one of Smith's former players and assistant coaches has been a 30-year osmosis.

In 1982, I wrote and published *March to the Top,* the story of Smith's first NCAA championship, and in 1985 my company, Four Corners Press, began putting out an annual on the Tar Heels called *Carolina Court.* Fortunately, in 1993, we were able to publish the national championship sequel, *Return to the Top.*

So a great deal of the research, anecdotes, and quotes for *The Dean's List* had already been compiled by myself and others on our staff.

Thus, I want to extend heartfelt acknowledgments to Alfred Hamilton, Jr., Ron Morris, and Lee Pace, who through the years have contributed informative, funny, and moving pieces on UNC games, players, and coaches for our publications, which also include *ACC Basketball: An Illustrated History,* written by Morris in 1988.

In addition, I have used material from *Carolina Court* stories written by David Glenn and my good friend Woody Durham, Voice of the Tar Heels. Dozens of newspaper and magazine stories and videos covering Carolina were also scanned for background.

The extraordinary collection of photos in this book come from a variety of sources, primarily Hugh Morton and Bob Donnan. The esteemed Mr. Morton, "governor" of Grandfather Mountain in Linville, N.C., has been taking pictures of special events at his alma mater since before I was born. At 75, he's as good as he ever was. Donnan shoots brilliant color action and candid basketball photos, annually risking his life to hang his strobe lights from the rafters of the Smith Center.

Other outstanding photos in *The Dean's List* were contributed by Sally Sather, Rich Clarkson, and the many photographers who have filled the files of the UNC Sports Information Office, completing what is unquestionably the definitive *pictorial* anthology of Smith's Tar Heel tenure as well.

Rick Wolff, senior editor at Warner Books, has been a driving force behind this project. The son of the famed baseball announcer and recent Hall of Fame inductee Bob Wolff, Rick navigated its publication with the same kind of care he uses in writing the acclaimed "Parents' Guide To Kids' Sports" series in *Sports Illustrated*. Rob McMahon, Wolff's editorial assistant, kept us all straight with his organizational excellence. Copy editor Fred Chase and production editor Mari Okuda made sure we were accurate on all names, numbers, and facts, and Howard Roberts's design speaks for itself.

On the home front, Linda Belans lent her eyes and ears, Jim Wilson was a master of grammar and punctuation, and Andy Diamondstein, one of the typically brainy out-of-state students at UNC, edited the overall manuscript so it would be understood by those who might not know as much about the Tar Heels as longtime die-hards.

The heart and soul of the book come from the actual Tar Heels, the players who have competed in Woollen Gym, Carmichael Auditorium, and the Smith Center over the past 35 years. Their personal recollections and testimonies about having worn the light blue, playing for a legendary coach, and representing UNC are, as the old saying goes, what it's all about. Special thanks go to Larry Brown, George Karl, and Jeff Lebo.

And, of course, there is Dean Smith, himself. Although he made it crystal clear from the beginning that he would not do an autobiography, Smith provided the private mailing list of his former players and managers so they would have a chance to contribute to the book. Always looking out for members of his extended family, Smith wanted to know if we intended to pay any of them.

I said we were on a very tight budget, but kidded him that we might be able to find a few hundred bucks for the guy who agreed to write the foreword.

"Ha, ha," said the man to whom *The Dean's List* is dedicated.

FOREWORD

Maybe I would still be a professional basketball player, but I am not sure how good I'd be or where I would be playing if I had not gone to Carolina and played for Dean Smith.

The two most important men in my life have been my father and Coach Smith. Now that my father is gone, Coach Smith fills that role in many ways—even more than 12 years after I left Chapel Hill.

I was a skinny, shy youngster when I first went to Carolina, not really secure about my basketball ability. Some people back home in Wilmington thought I should go to a smaller school where I could play for sure. My high school principal once suggested I go into the air force, so I could learn a skill and have a good job when I got out.

Fortunately, my parents emphasized schoolwork first, and they had confidence in my going to Carolina. From there, Coach Smith took over and helped me become the player and person I am today.

I will never forget my surprise when he put my name on the blackboard with the other starters before the Kansas game to begin my freshman year. I had missed a couple of weeks of preseason practice with an injured hand, and I had doubts that I could play with Sam Perkins and James Worthy.

In my three years of college, I learned more about playing basketball than running and dunking. I learned how to play defense, which helped me lead the NBA in steals and make the league's all-defensive team. I also learned the team concept, how to keep all five players involved and help them play up to their potential.

Jordan as a freshman hero of the 1982 NCAA champions.

I've heard a lot of people say that Coach Smith held me back, that he's the only person who could hold me to under a 20-point average. Well, I've got a secret for you: I averaged 20 as a sophomore! Seriously, I would never have been able to be the scorer, passer, rebounder, defender, or team player that I am without Coach Smith. Anyone who thinks otherwise just doesn't know anything about basketball.

He also showed his concern for me when he advised me to play professional basketball after my junior year, even though I was having a great time in college. He felt that it was the most opportune time to take the jump. That showed me an unselfish attitude on his part. I treasure that trait in him.

The only other person who wanted me to go was my roommate, Buzz Peterson, because he thought he would then get my starting position! I am only kidding about that, and Buzz is still one of my best friends in the world.

After I made my decision, Coach Smith didn't stop being my coach. He knew the Olympics were coming and that I needed to improve my ballhandling for Los Angeles and my rookie season. So he made me play point guard in our pick-up games that spring.

When my father was killed, Coach Smith and the rest of the Carolina family were there for me, my mother, brothers, and sisters. He met me at the Wilmington airport when I flew in for the funeral, and honestly I had been okay until I saw him. When I hugged him, I couldn't contain myself anymore.

Since then, he has been at the other end of the phone whenever I have needed him. Every once in a while I'll sneak into Chapel Hill and practice with the team or take him out to the golf course. He may be my coach and surrogate father, but he's as competitive in golf as he is in basketball. And though I hit the ball a lot farther, he usually gets it in the hole before I do.

Thanks for everything, Coach. I love you.

"Life must be lived forward but can only be
understood backward."
—*Søren Kierkegaard*

"You're only successful while you're succeeding."
—*Dean Smith*

"Nobody ever gets over being a Tar Heel."
—*Bill Currie*

Prologue:
Chasing the Baron

On a Thursday afternoon in August 1992, UNC assistant basketball coaches Phil Ford and Dave Hanners were playing golf with Eddie Fogler at the posh Governors Club, where Ford owned a home on the fifth tee. Fogler, the head coach at South Carolina and former long-time Tar Heel assistant, had never been to Ford's house and asked to see it when they finished playing.

During the golf there was light banter and heavy basketball talk. Ford confirmed the rumor that Jerry Stackhouse, the state's top high school basketball player as a junior, was coming to Chapel Hill that weekend for an unofficial visit. It was newsworthy, and a bit surprising, since recruiting speculation for months had predicted Stackhouse going to college somewhere else. Apparently, he was still looking at UNC.

After the round, they headed for Ford's luxurious home. Walking to one end of the house, they reached a study that had become a trophy room. Lined with mahogany paneling and glass cabinets, it was a tour through two decades of basketball greatness.

Among the hardware was Ford's array of prep honors from his decorated days at Rocky Mount High School: championship trophies and MVP plaques, pictures of games and the celebrations that ensued. Like Stackhouse, Ford had been considered the best player in the state.

One case held the Wooden Award given to Ford as the national collegiate Player of the Year in 1978, another the 1976 Olympic gold medal, a third the NBA Rookie of the Year trophy. Others had personal memorabilia, such as pictures of Ford with former UCLA coach John Wooden and his own college coach and current boss, Dean Smith.

As if it were a museum, Fogler was stone silent as he walked around the study, moving slowly from one exhibit to another. Finally, he turned to Ford and smiled.

"Phil, you know what you ought to do sometime?" he asked Ford, whom he had recruited and coached at Carolina. "Show Stackhouse this room, let him look around and then ask him just one question:

"'Do you think I would have these things, in this house, on this golf course, if I had played for any other college coach?'"

* * *

At some point in 1997, Dean Smith will win more games than any coach in the history of college basketball.

Unless he chooses to retire before breaking the record.

Trailing only the late and legendary Adolph Rupp, who won 876 games in 42 seasons at Kentucky, Smith owns 851 career victories as he enters the 1996–97 season, his 36th at the University of North Carolina.

However, there are few similarities in the eras in which both men worked, and the

"There are a few certainties in this life, but I've also learned that when March Madness rolls around Dean Smith's Tar Heels will always be there."
— President Bill Clinton, October 23, 1993, University Day Ceremonies at UNC

DEAN'S LIST

1993-94

No.	Name	Hgt.	Yr.	Hometown
00	Eric Montross	7' 0"	Sr.	Indianapolis, Ind.
4	Larry Davis	6' 3"	So.	Denmark, S.C.
5	Jeff McInnis	6' 3"	Fr.	Charlotte, N.C.
14	Derrick Phelps	6' 4"	Sr.	Pleasantville, N.Y.
21	Donald Williams	6' 3"	Jr.	Garner, N.C.
22	Pearce Landry	6' 5"	Jr.	Greensboro, N.C.
24	Dante Calabria	6' 4"	So.	Beaver Falls, Pa.
30	Rasheed Wallace	6' 10"	Fr.	Philadelphia, Pa.
31	Brian Reese	6' 6"	Sr.	Bronx, N.Y.
33	Kevin Salvadori	7' 0"	Sr.	Pittsburgh, Pa.
42	Jerry Stackhouse	6' 6"	Fr.	Kinston, N.C.
45	Serge Zwikker	7' 2"	Fr.	Maassluis, The Netherlands

Assistant Coaches: Bill Guthridge, Phil Ford, Dave Hanners

Ademola Okulaja (13) and Vince Carter (15), freshmen on the 1995–96 team.

differences between their coaching experiences make Smith's win total even more impressive than Rupp's.

Rupp's Kentucky teams dominated the basketball-weak Southeastern Conference from 1931 to 1972, winning 26 championships over schools that considered winter sports little more than recreation between football seasons. Basketball coaches at SEC schools often had other duties in the athletic department and university. Rupp, in the meantime, was a demigod—he occasionally invited game referees to ride with the Wildcats on road trips.

Smith, by contrast, has earned most of his victories over rivals in the Atlantic Coast Conference, long recognized as the most competitive collegiate basketball league. He coached through the start and full implementation of integration and, with teams that finished no lower than third in the ACC for the better part of four decades, has often been the target of opponents who were capable of beating his Tar Heels. Against all these obstacles, he has averaged 24 wins per season, compared to Rupp's 21.

And although Rupp won four national championships, one that he lost underscored how different *his* sport was at that time. In the 1966 NCAA title game, Texas Western's all-black starting five upset the all-white Wildcats. Once college basketball fully integrated, Rupp not only failed to win another national championship, he did not get back to the Final Four.

Smith's 26 invitations to the NCAA Tournament, 10 trips to the Final Four and two titles have resulted in an unmatched 61 tournament victories, 14 more than Wooden. Off the court, Smith's teams have never